From Average Dog

A practical four-week training guide for dogs and puppies

Sally Kilpatrick

Table of Contents

Foreword

I got into dog training when; finally, after years of wanting a dog, I finally got a gorgeous puppy. He was beautiful, but endlessly exuberant and quite a challenge. I took him to puppy school, where we didn't learn very much and I was convinced that there was a better way.

I eventually found a course that I did to become a qualified trainer myself. I did it through COAPE in the United Kingdom. The course allowed me to do what I love, and that is to learn as much as could about dog training!

Since then I have devoured many dog training and behaviour books, as well as scientific studies on methods of behaviour. I started my own dog school where I trained a few dogs over about three years.

I loved it. It made me better understand which dogs did best at training, and where things may go wrong and why. Since then I have trained several of my own dogs, not to competition standard, no one really needs that! But we have fun training and doing agility.

The most important thing I have learned over the years is that training is completely up to the owner. What you put in is what you get out. That synergy you see when someone has the best dog in the world, that is something they have worked towards.

And it is that sort of relationship anyone can have with his or her dog; I believe you can have it too, just practice.

Introduction

This is not as much about your dog, as it is about you. This guide aims to train you to train your dog and supply you with the tools that you need to train your dog, not only for the four weeks explained in this book, but for the lifetime of your dog.

Training your dog is one of the best relationship-building experiences that you will ever have with a companion animal. And it is a lot easier than it looks!

There are many different levels of training and although this book will help you with the most simple of tasks to ensure that you have a well-behaved dog, you can use the tools to take the training much further.

It is up to you! You may want to stop at simply getting your dog to sit on command, and to walk gently on a lead. Or you may want to teach him to fetch you a beer from the fridge, or to bring you the TV remote control whilst you stay on the couch. It is possible with the right mind-set and training tools.

In this four-week course each week will be building up on the preceding week and each of the week's exercises are designed to allow you to build up to more complex training. You will start simply, with a sit and build up on this through the four weeks until your dog will sit on command in as many places as possible.

Each week is designed to be followed step by step, and the training goals need to be reached before moving on to the next task. The aim of this book is to be simple, straightforward and practical and to deal with commonly encountered problems.

It is not meant as the ultimate training guide, nor as the one and only course you will ever need. But it will start you out on the right track, and make sure that you have the tools to train your dog to do pretty much anything.

Mind set and approach to training

Dog training is often viewed as complex and difficult, but it really isn't with a few simple tools. In this book the instructions given and the methods used are rewards-based training, which means one simple overarching rule:

Reward behaviours you do like, and ignore behaviours you don't like
In order to train your dog to the best of your ability there are a few things you need to master before you start.

This is all about mind-set. It may sound strange in the beginning, but if you do not have the correct mind-set when you begin, the training can be frustrating for you, and confusing for your dog. Importantly you must ensure that you do the following:

Do not get irritated with your dog during training!
You are welcome to call him all of the horrible names in the world, but you need to do it in an excited and high-pitched voice.

Remain calm
Your dog needs this. And it is a reiteration of the point above. If you get annoyed the training will be problematic for everyone!

Exercise your dog before training
You can take him for walk, or for a game of fetch at the park, or you can get the kids to run around with him for half an hour before your training session. This helps your dog to remain calm and focussed, and also helps to build your relationship with him.

Don't feed your dog before training

Try to feed him afterwards (twice a day, or three times if he is a puppy). This ensures that the treats you are going to use for training are extra delicious and appealing to your dog. Don't forget to feed him though!

Make it easy for your dog to get it right!
Training should be fun and rewarding for both you and your dog. Try not to push him too far beyond what he can do. Rather keep the challenges small and expand incrementally.

So don't try to get your dog to stay with you outside the room the first time you train it! Try to take baby steps, and always go back a step if your dog starts to get it wrong or gets confused.

Rewards-based training is the training method used most often today and is recommended by the best behaviourists.

What you have heard and what you should do: Eliminating confusion

There is a wealth of information out there on dog training, on the Internet, on the television and plenty of books. But how you know which method is best, and what you should do that is best for your dog?

Ideally, you should go back to the original training and behaviour research, and establish the facts in terms of what works and what doesn't for training.

But nobody really has time for that, so in this section is a summary of the most popular methods and training research. The summary will give you an idea of what works and what doesn't, and how to approach training your dog.

You can do quite a lot of reading on these subjects if you would like to explore it further. But, as this is a practical book of training, I have kept this section quite short.

1. But that guy on TV does it this way

TV dog trainers should not always be followed. They sometimes have no formal training in dog behaviour and training, and use pack and dominance-based theory.

You might be surprised to find that most qualified trainers do not approve of the methods used on some of TV's most popular dog shows. Not only should you seek professional help if your dog shows any sign of aggression, but you should never attempt to use the methods these trainers employ on TV at home.

These methods not only do not work in the long term, but also are not beneficial to you or your dog, and especially to your relationship with your dog.

The punishing techniques used by trainers following this system actually increase aggressive behaviour, and techniques such as forcing the dog onto its back and holding him down, grabbing the scruff of a dog's neck and others, result in aggressive responses in many cases.

Positive reinforcement and rehabilitation methods, however, show little aggressive responses. These can include rewarding your dog for making eye contact, teaching your dog to sit for anything he wants and exchanging items the dog has for treats.

And the results from science agree: positive reinforcement is better.

The dominance theory, which has been used in dog training for quite some time, is based on research done on captive wolf packs. The theory has been discredited in recent years for dog training based on results of dog behaviour research.

It has been shown to cause fearful reactions and behaviour in dogs, a response that often results in aggression. Besides that, the basic premise of the theory is not useful for dog training.

The theory is based on wolf packs, but not only were these wolf packs captive, they were also composed of several members from different family groups.

Aside from the fact that this is a very unnatural system for wolves (being both captive, and not within their normal family pack environment) but wolves are not dogs. In fact research has shown that in natural wolf packs, dominance behaviour and challenges are rarely displayed.

The lessons learned during the research on wolves are not only inapplicable to natural wolf packs, but is definitely not applicable to domestic dogs. Trying to become the "pack leader" is thus a bit pointless and irrelevant.

The emphasis here is on developing a good relationship with your dog, and pack theory does not form part of that.

2. Apparently it's my fault

Yes it is. You train you dog and he learns his responses and behaviours from you. There are studies that have been done that prove this. Inconsistency in training is one of the big reasons why training certain behaviours fail. Consistency is perhaps the most important aspect of training.

A good example of where this works is in teaching your dog not to jump up. Most dogs do, they want to greet you when you get home and for them this means jumping up and licking your face.

This kind of behaviour, though, is never acceptable to people (unless you have a very small dog, small dogs tend to get away with many more behaviour issues than large dogs).

The ways in which to stop your dog from jumping up are overall quite simple; you have to ignore the behaviour. Consistently. And that means no scolding, no kneeing your dog in the chest and no eye contact.

The best way to deal with jumping is to fold your arms, turn away from your dog and look up to the sky. To reinforce this, you may only greet your dog when he is sitting.

Your dog will quickly learn that he will get attention when sitting, but none when jumping and will stop jumping. However, if this is not consistent, your dog will not understand and the behavioural issue will never be resolved.

And by consistent, every single member of the family and all visitors need to follow the same procedure. Your dog should always be treated in this way.

This is simply demonstrated by a couple that joined my dog classes. They had a lovely dog, a crossbreed about knee high. One of their problems, aside from doing basic training, was that their dog jumped up all the time.

I gave them the advice above and we practiced a few times, I also made sure that they understood that consistency is important.

A couple of weeks later they came to me and complained that the training was not working. We discussed it, and they promised me that they were being consistent, and all visitors to their house were following the same process.

As we were discussing this, their dog was jumping up and both owners were absentmindedly stroking her ears.

This is clear inconsistency and the dog was being rewarded for the behaviour! She would of course continue to jump if the owners continued to reward her for it.

After pointing it out to them, they became more aware of their dog's behaviour and applied the methods consistently to great effect. It is incredibly important that you are consistent!

Another aspect of this problem is that many people find that when they come home, their dog may cower or hide in a corner, or both. Although many people attribute this to their dog "knowing" he has done something wrong, it is far simpler than that.

You may have left your dog at home for an extended period of time, a time in which he got bored.

He probably found some ways to deal with his boredom, which could have involved digging up and chewing your entire irrigation system, digging several holes in the garden, chewing your favourite deck chair, uprooting the rose bush your mother gave you last birthday or several other fun adventures.

Your dog probably did this a while ago, and had an enormous amount of fun, but when you come home you punish him for it.

Not only are you teaching your dog nothing about abstaining from the behaviour, you are very effectively teaching him that when you come home, he will be punished.

So the association for him is not digging=punishment but rather owner coming home=punishment. So he may have done something naughty, but his cowering has nothing to do with it.

Dogs are unable to associate punishment with the behaviour unless punishment is given in the middle of the dog engaging in that behaviour. But even direct punishment is problematic, with your dog more likely to associate the punishment with you coupled with the behaviour, rather than just the behaviour.

And punishment in such a way trains your dog to refrain from that behaviour, but only when you are around. So your dog will stop digging, when you are there to see it, and continue to do it when you are not. This really doesn't resolve the behaviour. Which is why one of the cardinal rules in rewards-based training is to ignore behaviour you don't like.

Problems associated with bored dogs, such as digging, excessive barking, destruction of gardens, chewing, can easily be solved by engaging your dog in activities.

Playtime, exercise, and the provision of plenty of toys that help keep your dog busy will reduce this behaviour. And, if your dog is a puppy, you will find that he often will grow out of these sorts of behaviours.

1. How come that old lady's dog is so good?

Chances are that the old lady to whom you are referring is retired and spends all her time at home. She might even live alone, with her only companion her dog. This means she spend a great deal of time with her dog.

So you, who are at work all day and lifting kids here and there and only getting home late at night cannot even begin to spend as much time with your dog as the old lady does with hers.

You probably then have a lot less time to engage with your dog, and to spend time with him, and to spend time training him. The result is that yes, that old lady's dog is much better behaved than yours.

Not only does he not dig because he has constant human companionship, but your old lady spends time with him playing, or talking to him and training and walking him.

All of these activities mean that they have a great relationship, and her dog has learned all of her signals and what she wants through both active and passive training and reinforcement.

The more time you spend with your dog, the better your relationship with him will be. And active time is better than passive time: taking Rex for a walk will enable both you and him to develop a better relationship than when he lies at your feet whilst you watch TV.

The more of this time that you can fit into your day, the better your relationship with your dog will be. This is because short training sessions are recommended each day and another reason why you should walk your dog every day.

What you get in is what you get out. You may never be able to put in as much as that old lady does, but you can build a great relationship with your dog.

Preparation

Each training session should be no longer than 15 minutes, and can be even shorter if you have a puppy. But do make sure that you have at least two training session per day, and up to four if you can.

Try for before breakfast and before supper, and, if you can, at lunchtime and when you get home from work. The more training sessions you can get in, the better and the faster your dog will learn.

Make sure that for each training session you have enough treats available. These should be in an easy to reach area but out of the way of your dog, you don't want him stealing all the treats in the middle of the training session! Treats should be something that your dog enjoys.

You can use cold meats, cheese, chicken, and meat, even bread but make sure that the treats are soft (so that your dog can eat them quickly) and cut very small (so they are really just a taste).

One treat should be the size of half your baby fingernail or even smaller if you have a very small dog breed such as a Pekinese or a puppy. Also make sure your dog loves the treats, some dogs refuse to eat cheese and others love it. It is important that your dog loves his rewards.

Make sure that you have no distractions for the training sessions, especially if you have a puppy. Dogs don't have the best attention spans and you need your dog to have his attention on you throughout the training time.

After the initial training, you can challenge your dog by increasing the levels of distractions, but that will come at a later stage!

Exercise your dog before the training session. Even 15 minutes of playtime will get rid of excess energy and have him ready to listen to you. If you have a puppy under 6 months, make sure to exercise him carefully.

Small puppies should not go on long walks (over 15 minutes), as it is bad for bone growth and development.

You should have a collar and lead. Make sure that the collar is an ordinary collar, no choke chains or check chains! Your dog is unlikely to need such devices and if he does, you should probably call in a professional to help.

You will have to hold onto the lead for the duration of the training sessions, and use it in some so make sure that you have one.

If you are training before breakfast or dinner, make sure that you have your dog's meal ready for after training, he will definitely be hungry. And ensure that there is always fresh clean water available for your dog.

So, in order to prepare for your session, make sure that you have the following:

15 minutes of uninterrupted time in a quiet place;
A calm, exercised dog;
Plenty of treats;
Collar and lead; and

Your dog's breakfast or dinner (or lunch of you have a puppy) for after the training session.

Fundamentals

There are a few fundamental things that you will have to make sure that you are able to do properly before you begin training. If you master them, you are sure to be successful in training.

For the purposes of this four-week course, a clicker is not necessary and it really is easier if you don't use one at this stage. If you would like to use one, you should get a professional dog trainer to help you learn how to use it properly.

For this four-week course we will be dealing with simple voice commands and treats, of course.

1. Use of "good dog"

You need to make sure that you reward your dog properly. It is quite difficult for a dog to learn how to sit if he is a bit uncertain as to what a sit is. You can make sure that he knows.

We shall use "sit" as the example. If you ask your dog to sit, and he does so, there are several steps to get to that point. He may step back, and then lower his bum to the floor slowly, all the time waiting for his treat.

But the actual "sit" is when his bum touches the floor. That is the moment your dog needs to recognise as "sit" and it is at this exact moment that you should praise your dog.

The treat can follow shortly afterwards, just make sure you say "good dog!" at exactly the right moment. The same must be done for "down" where the exact moment that your dog's belly touches the floor is the down and when you should say "good dog!" This is very important.

You dog can only know the right thing to do when you reward him at the right time. You may find that at first he is uncertain but he will soon figure it out!

2. Use of the treats

In this type of training treats are essential. They give your dog something to work towards. You do need to get the treats right though, as not all dogs are the same.

Some careful experimentation will help you to discover which treats work best for your dog. Some dogs adore cheese others hate it. So experiment, and try to find something that your dog really loves!

You may find that treats are not at all appealing to your dog. But this is not too much of a problem as something else may be. Although treats are by far the easiest way to train a dog, training can be done with a ball or other toy as a reward, or even just a really good tummy scratch!

If you have to use something other than treats though, try to use a toy and make sure that your dog will relinquish it once the reward is over. You should allow only a few seconds of play as a reward for getting something right. But for now, all rewards will be called treats.

Treats must be used every single time in the beginning. After that, we can introduce a way of weaning your dog off treats every time. But for now, your dog should be getting a treat every single time he does something right. Treats generally follow the "good dog" that mark the exact moment your dog got it right.

Try to make sure he gets his treat in the next minute or so and make sure that you always give him one. It helps to have treats nearby at all times and a few in your handbag or briefcase and pockets won't go amiss.

3. Practice

As with everything, practice makes perfect. The more you practice, the better your dog will get. Some of the world's most famous dogs may practice up to 5 hours a day! You definitely get what you put in.

If you are training a puppy, it is likely that his attention span will not last much longer than 15 minutes at most so try not to push it to hours at a time!

It is recommended that several short training sessions be done each day, rather than one long one. It helps your dog to keep interested, and it prevents you from getting annoyed if his attention wavers.

You should be managing at least two training sessions per day, ideally one in the morning before you feed your dog his breakfast, and another in the evening before you feed your dog his dinner.

If you have an older dog (over 6 months) you can increase the training times, but more short sessions are more beneficial than fewer longer sessions.

4. The Build Up

Dog training is based on building up behaviours from very simple beginnings. It is important to follow the guide to achieve the best results and to make sure that neither you, nor your dog, are frustrated.

Make sure that you complete one stage before moving on to the next. And make sure you are able to do each of the tasks before moving onto the next steps.

The more you practice, the easier it will become and the faster you can proceed.

5. Always end on a good note

It is very important that training sessions are fun and enjoyable for both you and your dog. To make sure that your dog enjoys his training, and is happy to do it with you, always make sure that you end on a good note. Ideally this should be something that your dog can do without any problem at all, 100 % of the time.

If your dog can sit, then end on the sit. Ask him to sit, and when he does give him lots of praise and a treat, or several, and end the session. If your dog can't sit yet, there is an exercise in Week One called Attention. Your dog will be able to do this quickly, so end on that for the first few sessions until he can do a sit happily.

Training Program – Week One

In this week you will learn some of the foundations of training, and start easy. This is the week you will first teach your dog to love your training sessions, so make sure that you remain upbeat.

Keep the training session short (ten to fifteen minutes) and try to fit at least two into your day, more if you can! Remember to have treats ready and to begin in an area of minimal distractions.

This week you will learn how to train the attention, which is one of the most important exercises, and how to sit. You will also be learning one of the tricks of dog training, which is how to use a lure to train your dog.

Using a lure makes the training quick and easy and you will find that your dog responds well if it is done correctly.

There are a few exercises that you can begin now and continue to train throughout the weeks of the course and beyond. You will find these in Other Activities chapter.

It is a good idea to read that chapter now so that you may begin those simple tasks, which are not restricted to the training sessions, you will do for each week. They will also be briefly explained each week but these tasks can fall into other time that you spend with your dog, not only the training sessions.

1. Attention

The attention is the first step to most training. What it does, at the very basic level, is teach your dog his name. Further than that, it is the start of the recall, as well as the start of just getting his attention.

This exercise trains your dog to look at you every time you call his name. It also introduces your dog to training and makes it easy for him to get it right from the beginning.

After a few practices of this exercise your dog will know that you are training, and that training is fun! He learns that treats will come if he does what you ask and you will find that he starts to recognise when it is training time, and he may even get excited.

You will need to begin by holding a treat in your hand. It doesn't matter if your dog is paying you any attention at this stage. He probably is a little confused. The first step is easy; say your dog's name (preferably in a high pitched happy voice – dogs respond best to that kind of voice).

The goal is to get your dog to look at you. In the beginning, if he looks in your general direction, that's ok. As soon as he does, say an excited "good boy!" followed by a treat.

The goal here is to get your dog to look at your face when you call his name. We can easily reach that point in the first training session. Here is when the lure first comes into play. When your dog is consistently looking in your direction, and you are treating him each time, try to make it a little more difficult.

Now, when you call him, not only should he be looking in your direction, he should be looking at you. So when he looks at you, give him a treat. When he is consistently looking at you, then you can increase the difficulty level once again.

Now try to get him to look at your face when you call his name. This might be quite difficult for your dog, as he is likely to want to look at the treat, rather than you.

If he does this, then hold the treat up to the side of your face. This will encourage him to look in the right direction. When he glances at you, rather than at the treat, then praise him happily and give him the treat.

You may need to continue this for a few times before he realizes that you want him to look at you, rather than at the treat. He will get there so keep persevering!

Once your dog is looking at your face consistently, try to move the treat away from your face. He may take a while to realize that you still want him to look at you, so make sure that you do it slowly, increasing the distance your hand is from your face only by tiny amounts.

Eventually, you should work towards him looking at you without you having a treat in your hand (but nearby, so you can give it to him when he gets the exercise right).

For this week, try to get your dog to look at your face consistently, even if he can only do it if you have a treat in your hand close to your face. Practice this every day.

If your dog gets confused, or you try to move to fast, then simply go back a step and try to get him to do that step consistently until you try to move on again.

So, the **steps** you will follow for this week for the Attention will be:

1. Make sure that you are in an area without any distractions with plenty of treats.

2. Call your dog's name. When he looks in your direction praise him and give him a treat.
3. Make sure he looks in your direction consistently before moving on to the next step.

4. Call your dog's name; try to get him to look at you (not just in your general direction), and when he does, praise him and give a treat.

5. Make sure that he completes the previous step consistently before moving on to the next step.

6. Call your dog's name; try to get him to look at your face (not just you). When he does, praise him and give him a treat.

7. Practice! Practice! Practice! This is how you will begin each and every training session. You will also be ending each training session in this way until your dog can sit consistently.

Sit

The sit is one of the easiest tasks to teach a dog. It is taught using a lure and is very simple. One thing that you should bear in mind for this exercise (and the others that follow) is that dogs are very bad at generalizing.

This means that if you teach your dog to sit in the kitchen, and only practice in the kitchen, your dog will have learned that sit means to sit in the kitchen.

It is unlikely that he will generalize the term to mean sit anywhere. So he will be unlikely to sit outside, or in the park, or even in the lounge. During the four-week course you will teach the sit, and then practice it in as many locations as possible. But for this week, lets concentrate on getting it right all of the time.

Once you have completed the Attention exercises (remember to keep your training session short and easy), you can move on to the sit. Even if your dog already sits, it will be a good idea to follow this section of the training in order to give him some more practice.

The sit can be taught using voice commands, but it is also useful to use a hand signal. The hand signal for sit is to hold your hand out, palm up, and move it from the starting position from next to your hips to about waist high. You will not start teaching the sit from standing upright, but you will end up there!

Begin the sit by kneeling next to your dog with a treat in your hand. Hold the treat in your hand just above his nose (but make sure he cannot get it from you). Once he knows where the treat is he should follow it with his nose. Now move the treat horizontally over his back a little way.

Don't lift the treat up, or he will jump backwards! Your dog's nose should follow the treat and you will find he sits to reach it. Once he sits (bum touches the ground) praise him and give him the treat.

Remember that the praise must come as he sits, not before or after! If you can, you can hold the treat in your hand flat, palm up so that the lure you are giving your dog is the hand signal for sit.

You will need to practice this several times, and you may need to get your dog to get up between sits as he may not understand why he can't continue sitting and just get treats!

The more you practice, the better your dog will become. Keep doing this until your dog is sitting consistently. You can then add the "sit" command. You can say this at the beginning of the sit when the lure is still above your dog's nose.

Once your dog is sitting with the lure consistently, you may want to try to remove it. You will still treat your dog when he gets it right, but try to keep the treat in your other hand. This may take a little time for him to get right, but keep trying; he will learn that he will still get a treat.

Make sure that you retain the hand signal and the "sit" command. The next few weeks we will build on this.

In order to proceed to the next week, make sure you are able to get your dog to sit on command (with the hand signal) with the treat either in your other hand or within reach nearby. You can still be kneeling in front of your dog at this point.

The **steps** that you will need to follow for the Sit for this week are:

1. The sit follows on from the attention, so you will still need to be in an area without distractions and with plenty of treats;

2. Kneel in front of your dog with a treat in your hand;

3. Make sure that the treat cannot be snatched from you by your dog and try to hold your hand flat with your palm up;

4. Hold the treat above your dog's nose and slowly move your hand horizontally over your dog's back whilst saying "sit"

5. As soon as your dog's bum touches the ground, praise him and give him the treat

6. Practice this several times and when your dog is consistently sitting, put the treat in your other hand and continue asking for the sit without the lure, make sure that you still praise him and give him the treat when he gets it right

7. Keep practicing!

8. If you find your dog is happy to sit with the hand signal and command, then you can try to practice the sit in other places, but make sure that you always give a treat!

Some words of caution:

Your dog might only sit if you are kneeling near him, that's ok for now. You will need to be patient, especially if you have a puppy, to make sure you do not push your dog too far. If he battles with a step, then go back a step and keep going.

Make sure that you begin and end each session with the attention exercises. The more practice you get with these the better. You may end each session with a sit if you would like, but make sure that your dog is able to do it successfully each time so that you will always end on a good note!

Training Program – Week Two

You should have managed to fit in at least seven training sessions last week and your dog should be consistently looking at your face when you call his name and sitting when you ask him to. Well done! If you have achieved this then you are ready to move on. If not, then keep practising until you can.

Don't push your dog too far at once. You should be practicing the attention and the sit in each training session. Don't forget to practice both exercises, as they are important!

Sit

If you have been working consistently at the sit for the past week, your dog is probably doing it with few problems. One problem you may have encountered, however, is that your dog can only sit when you are kneeling in front of him.

This is fairly common so don't worry! We simply have to work at getting him to understand that when you say sit and use the hand signal whilst standing, it means the same thing.

The process to follow is to stand up in increments and make sure that your dog does the site at each of the different increments. So start by kneeling upright, and using the command and hand signal to ask for the sit. When your dog is doing this consistently, then get up a little more, such as in a crouch.

Again get your dog to do the sit and make sure that he does it consistently before moving on. Eventually, he will be sitting happily when you ask him whilst standing.

If he can't master the sit at any of your levels, then try to go back a step and try again. Or you may be getting up a little fast for him, in which case try to make the increments a bit smaller.

In doing this exercise you have achieved one of the most important aspects of dog training, which is using incremental changes to advance the behaviour. This can be done for a variety of more complex tasks.

If your dog is already doing the sit when commanded from standing, then you can move on to slightly more complex tasks. Ask your dog to sit in as many places as possible.

You will still have to give him a treat, and you will still have to make sure he is not distracted when you ask him to sit, but you are now building his knowledge that sit means sit, no matter where he is.

It is important that you only ask your dog to sit when he is not distracted. If you ask him when he is busy running around, or greeting another dog, or sniffing a puddle you are only teaching him that ignoring you is ok.

You can also work on the timing of the sit. You might find that your dog takes a while to get into the correct position. Praising him when he does it quickly will train him to do it faster.

You may also want to work with other members of your family. This can be done as well, so long as it is approached in a calm and controlled manner.

So the **steps** to follow are:

1. Build up small incremental changes into the training for sit, do this by slowly getting up whilst asking your dog to sit in a series of 5 to 10 different positions. Make sure that your dog completes the first increment consistently before moving onto the next.

2. Ask your dog to sit in as many different places as possible. But make sure you always have a treat, and that the distraction levels are low.

3. Different members of your family can ask your dog to sit, make sure the command is always clear, there is always a treat and that the environment is calm and controlled (no dog will be able to sit if two loud children are trying to cuddle him at the same time).

Down

In my experience down is actually one of the most challenging commands to train and it may take a while. Persistence and patience is key here. You may well need the whole week to make sure that you get it right. The easiest method is with the lure, which we have already used for both the attention and the sit.

Very small dogs may not really understand the down, if you feel no need to train the down then your dog is very likely to pick up on it. It is very useful and great practice for you to develop some training techniques so I recommend you do not give it a skip.

You will need to get your dog to sit to start off with (something he should be good at by now). You will need a treat in your hand. The hand signal for the down is a flat hand, with palm down that is brought down from the starting position by the waist, to next to the thigh.

This is what you should aim for when using the lure. Just make sure that your dog cannot snatch the treat from your hand when you teach him the down! You can hold the treat level with his nose when he is sitting. You then bring your hand directly down in-between your dog's front paws.

Don't move your hand forward as your dog is likely to jump forward to get the treat. He may be confused at first, but give him a few chances. The lure should draw his nose to the treat and he should lie down to reach it. The moment he lies down, praise him and let him have the treat!

You will need to practice this several times before your dog understands what you want but he will soon get it. Be sure to persevere and stay patient.

When your dog is lying down consistently, then you can add the "down" command. Make sure that he is doing it consistently before moving onto the next step. It might take you a few sessions to get your dog to understand what down means.

Be patient and keep going! And make sure that you end the session with something he can do, like attention, or sit. Your goal for down for this week is to get your dog to do it consistently every time. We will start to work towards getting rid of the lure next week.

The **steps** to follow for the down are:

1. Make sure you are in an area with few distractions and plenty of treats

2. Get your dog to sit

3. Take a treat in your hand and hold it level with your dog's nose

4. Slowly lower the treat to the ground between your dog's front paws

5. Your dog will lie down to get the treat

6. Praise him and let him have the treat

7. Once he is lying down consistently, then you can add the "down" command

8. Practice! Practice! Practice!

Some words of caution:

Only ask your dog to do something when he is focussed on you. He then has the best opportunity to get it right, and will not learn to ignore you.

Do not repeat the command. Repeating the command "sit" several times teaches your dog to ignore you. The trick is to ask him when he is focussed on you, and only once.

Training Program – Week Three

You should have managed to fit in at least seven training sessions last week and your dog should be consistently looking at your face when you call his name, sitting on command wherever you are, and lying down happily.

Well done! If you have achieved this then you are ready to move on. If not, then keep practising until you can.

Don't push your dog too far at once. You should be practicing the attention, sit and down in each training session. Don't forget to practice all three, as they are important!

Sit

At this stage, your sit should be getting pretty good. If you have managed to practice it in a number of different places then that is excellent!

The overall training for the sit is the process you will follow for each of your training exercises, where we will learn the exercise, practice it in as many places as possible, and then reinforce it following a new treating procedure.

Now that your dog is sitting on command and in as many places as possible, but with a treat each and every time, then we can start to get rid of the treat.

In truth, you will never completely get rid of the treat as your dog will always need treats throughout his life to reinforce the behaviour but what we will do this week is to try to wean your dog off a treat each and every time.

What we will be learning this week for the sit is what trainers call an intermittent reinforcement schedule. It works in the same way gambling works, essentially.

You may not win each and every time, but the possibility of winning means that you will continue playing. It is similar for dogs and we will even be giving your dog a jackpot every now and again.

With this treat schedule, you will start by giving your dogs treats most of the time, with a few times when you don't reward with a treat. The trick is to try to do it randomly. Every now and again, instead of giving your dog just one treat for getting it right, you may want to give him 10.

This type of treat schedule means that your dog never knows when a treat is coming, and when it does, that it might be a jackpot! In this way, you still reinforce his behaviour, but without having to treat each and every time.

You can even reduce the treats quite substantially, but not completely. And make sure that you do not do this too quickly, or your dog will stop sitting! So try the intermittent reinforcement schedule this week with the sit.

Down

After last week your dog should be able to do a down, but, as with the sit, he is likely doing it only when you are kneeling on front of him. For this week, slowly work towards asking for a down whilst standing, as we did with the sit.

Get up incrementally and ensure that your dog is doing a down consistently before you move once again. If at any point your dog gets a little confused and will not do the down, then go back a step.

It should take you most of the week to reach this point but be patient, and keep practicing!

The **steps** to follow are the same as for the sit, but here they are again:

1. Build up small incremental changes into the training for down, do this by slowly getting up whilst asking your dog to down in a series of 5 to 10 different positions. Make sure that your dog completes the first increment consistently before moving onto the next.

2. Ask your dog to down in as many different places as possible. But make sure you always have a treat, and that the distraction levels are low.

3. Different members of your family can ask your dog to down, make sure the command is always clear; there is always a treat and that the environment is calm and controlled (no dog will be able to do any exercises if two loud children are trying to cuddle him at the same time).

Sit and Down exercises

Doggy sit-ups are one of the most entertaining exercises for both you and your dog, and will teach your dog to do them quickly and on command as well allowing you to practice the intermittent reinforcement introduced last week.

Once your dog is sitting and downing easily, you can get him to do a series of sit-down-sit-down-sit-down. You can do these exercises in as many places as possible, and as often as possible. You may want to also introduce the stay into the mix as well otherwise your dog will soon get the hang of it and anticipate your commands. Try to make sure he only sits and downs on your command!

Stay

The stay is the next step in the training schedule and something else to do this week. Again, it needs to be built up so this week we will start out easy! Get your dog to sit. Now, to begin with drop the lead (if you hang onto it he might follow you!). Ask him to stay. You may use a hand signal for this, which usually your hand is facing forward with palm out towards your dog, like you would if you were showing someone to stop. Take a small step back. The goal in these initial phases is to make it easy for your dog to get it right.

He may take a while to understand, as this is a new exercise. Make sure you reward him when he gets it right so that he learns what you want. Then you can start building it up. So begin with one step, stay facing your dog. If he manages to stay for a count of 5 (do the counting in your head) then praise him, call him to you and reward him. This not only teaches the stay, but also reinforces the recall.

When he starts to get this small stay right all of the time you can build up to the next step. Build up the steps slowly, you may want to start with distance, so increase the distance between you until you can do a stay 10 steps away for a count of 5 continually. When you have achieved this, you can increase the time of the stay from a count of 5 to a count of 10, all the way up to a minute.

You will find this quite easy to achieve and your dog will find it quite a bit of fun! The stay is a lot of fun to teach as you can keep on building it up.

A recap of the **steps** you will follow is here:

1. Ask your dog to sit and then tell him to stay.

2. Take one step away from your dog, but keep facing him. If he manages to stay for a count of 5 praise him and give him a treat.

3. Increase the amount of time that you ask your dog to stay incrementally. You can build this up to a few minutes. Make sure he is able to do it consistently each time before moving on to the next step.

4. You can also increase the distance, stay facing your dog but increase the number of steps you take each time.

5. For this week try to aim for a 1-minute stay at 20 steps away.

A few words of caution:

Remember to move slowly in little steps that your dog can do, moving from a one-step-away 10-second stay is a very long way away from a 1 minute stay so be patient.

You are by now using intermittent reinforcement with your sit, which is great, and you will begin to use this for other exercises, but whenever you teach a new exercise, you will need to stick to the original treating schedule: 1 treat each and every time.

Training Program – Week Four

By now you and your dog should be sitting, downing, happily doing puppy push-ups and doing a very reasonable stay. Make sure that you still practice the attention as well.

At this stage try to get out and about practicing what you have learned in as many places as possible. You should know what treats your dog responds best to, and that look he gets when he suddenly knows what it is that you are asking him to do. Keep at it!

The tools that you have learned this week can be used to train all sorts of tricks! For week four, we will be looking at increasing the challenge of the stay, as well as enforcing the sit and down.

Sit

Continue what you are doing! By now the sit should be as easy as breathing for you and your dog. Keep using the intermittent reinforcement schedule, but you can probably reduce the frequency of treating quite substantially by now. Keep sitting in as many places as possible.

Show off your sit to friends and family. You can also ask your dog to sit for any number of things; it's a good general rule to have. He can sit before you open the door for him, he can sit before he gets his dinner, before you go on walks. The more you practice, the better he will get.

Down

By now the down should be getting easier. It will never be as easy as the sit unless you practice it as much so from this week onwards you will continue to practice the down.

When your dog is doing it continually when asked, then you can introduce the intermittent reinforcement schedule as you did with the sit. Don't forget to practice!

Sit and down exercises

Keep doing those puppy push-ups! And try to do them in as many places as possible. It is also a fun trick to show off to friends. The more you practice, the better your dog will get. Also if you can add a few stays into the mix then your dog won't know what's coming so the challenge will be increased.

Stay

The stay can be built up somewhat from last week. Hopefully you have managed to build up to a point where your dog will stay for a minute at 20 steps away. Well done! That is excellent.

Now what you will need to try and do is to be able to ask your dog to stay and to walk away from him with your back to him. This is more challenging for your dog as he would rather be with you but keep trying. Remember to build it up slowly to achieve what you want to achieve.

As your dog now knows what stay is, it should be easier to increase the challenge for him. Initially, you may want to ask him to stay and simply turn your back on him. You will probably need a friend for this exercise, as you will not be able to keep an eye on your dog all the time to check up what he is doing.

Start by asking your dog to stay and turning your back on him. If he stays for a count of 5, then praise him and give him a treat. Then you can begin slowly building up the distance and the time that you ask him to stay. This can be done the same way you built up time and distance last week.

The biggest challenge for the stay will be getting your dog to stay when you are busy doing something. A good challenge is to try to walk circles around your dog whilst he is staying.

You may need to build this up slowly as well. He should learn that stay means he must stay no matter what is happening. So increase the challenge for him by increasing your movement, (slowly! And for only a few seconds at first) whilst he is in the stay position.

You can also challenge him even more by getting him to stay when you leave the room. Make sure that you increase these challenges extremely slowly. Once he has mastered each step, you can introduce the intermittent reinforcement schedule.

So the steps for this week are something that you can continue to work on:

1. Get your dog to stay with your back to him, get a friend to help and start slowly simply with your back to him

2. Increase the distance you ask your dog to stay with your back to him

3. Increase the time you ask your dog to stay with your back to him

4. Increase the challenge for the stay by increasing your movement, or trying for the stay when you are out of the room.

Some words of caution:

Remember that you should only proceed slowly: build up the exercise. Don't ask your dog to stay whilst you dance around him when the last exercise he got right was to stay with you 5 steps away. Slow and patient is the key to building up behaviour.

Train the tricks in the Other Activities chapter and, once you have the basics you will be able to train anything!

Other activities

House Training

House training is one of the early challenges of puppy ownership, and may even be something you may have to train an adult dog of you are lucky enough to adopt a rescue dog.

It is probably the most essential training you will ever do with your dog, and it is very easy. You can do it with a careful mix of timing and rewards. The method that I describe here is tried and tested and extremely successful:

1. Take your puppy outside immediately after eating, and about an hour after eating. You may find that you begin to recognize when your puppy usually needs to go, and this tends to be between immediately after and up to 2 hours after eating.

2. Take your puppy out every two hours. Puppies need to wee a lot, so make sure that you give your dog plenty of opportunities to do so. The more you take him out, the more of an opportunity he has to get it right.

3. Once your dog does a poo or wee, praise him enthusiastically and give him a treat. You may find you do not always have treats at hand. It is fine if you don't reward your puppy, but it will go much faster if you do!

4. At night, it is a good idea to let your puppy sleep in your bed. Puppies won't wee and poo in their bed, they move out of it to do so. So your puppy will most likely wake you up when he needs to go outside. He also might want to play at this point.

If your puppy wakes you up at night pick him up (no cuddles or talking or playing), put him outside, wait for him to poo or wee and praise him and give him a treat.

Then pick him up again (still no talking or attention) and go back to bed. Ignore him wanting to play with you! This is also part of teaching your puppy to sleep through the night.

5. Remember, puppies are like babies; they will not be able to make it through the whole night until they are old enough. Be patient with your puppy, he may need between 4 and 6 months before he can get through a night without waking you to be let out.

6. Make sure that your puppy has access to outside! If he doesn't, he might have accidents in the house only because he couldn't get outside!
7. Rubbing his nose in it will not teach him anything, please don't do this. If you find a mess inside clean it up with ammonia free cleaning product and don't discipline your dog.

If you catch him in the middle of doing a poo or wee, pick him up straight away and put him outside. If he finishes up outside then huge praise and a treat!

If you consistently follow the advice then your dog should have very few accidents inside and will be house trained in no time. If you have an adult dog, the same applies. It may take a little longer for adult dogs though, so be patient.

Do remember that if you discipline your dog for doing a wee or poo inside the house when he is doing it you are not teaching him not to have accidents in the house, you are teaching him not to do a wee or poo when you can see him. You don't want to teach him that!

Walking loosely on a lead

Walking loosely on a lead is one of the most important things you can teach your dog, especially if you have a large breed. It is also one of the most difficult things to teach and takes a great deal of patience coupled with a lot of practice.

You may have noticed that your dog walks much better on lead once he is halfway through your walk. This is because, as usually, a tired dog is a good dog. Before training your dog on lead, it is a good idea to try to get him a little tired.

So try fifteen minutes of playtime, or fifteen minutes of off lead walking to get him a little more tired.

Then the training can begin! First of all you will need your dog on a collar and lead and you will need to be relatively calm. It is a good idea to start this training in a controlled environment where there are few distractions and certainly no squirrels for your dog to chase.

Try to get your dog to be relaxed as well. You may want to have a few treats in your hand, and make sure that your dog knows that they are there. This will make sure that his attention is on you, and not on what is going on around him.

In obedience training, your dog needs to be on a specific side but for this exercise, any side will do.

Hold the lead in the hand opposite the side your dog is on so that it crosses in front of your body. It is a good idea to hold a few treats in your hand closest to your dog and make sure that he knows they are there! If he is focussed on the treats, he is less likely to pull.

You may then begin walking. If your dog pulls, as soon as the lead become taunt, stop walking. Just stop and stand still. You will find that once your dog has continued to pull for a while, he will turn around and look at you.

At this point, the lead should go slack. When the lead goes slack, you can call your dog to you and give him a treat, and then continue walking.

You will need to repeat this several times, and may even only walk a few metres in the first half an hour that you practice this exercise. But you will get there if you persevere. You are teaching your dog that pulling gets him nowhere, but that walking with a slack lead means he can continue to walk and that he gets treats.

Now, here is where it really tests your patience. You will have to practice this exercise EVERY TIME your dog is on lead. That means you have to do it when you take him to the vet, or try to get him into the car to go to the beach.

It is important that you are consistent in this exercise otherwise your dog will not learn.

You may be tempted to use tools like choke chains. Choke chains have been shown to be a health hazard for dogs, especially when used on dogs that pull and many suffer from damaged trachea and other problems as a result.

There are also several brands of non-pull halters and harnesses that you can get for your dog. They work and are not harmful to your dog. You may use these if your dog's pulling is a major problem, but bear in mind they will not teach your dog to walk loosely on a normal collar and lead.

The recall

This is another of the most important things that you can teach your dog, and it is something you will need to teach them to ensure that you can call them when they chase a bicycle, or a squirrel, or small children.

It is also essential for calling your dog back if he is in danger. This section will give you some exercises to do to make sure that your dog learns to come when called. You can work on this throughout the four-week course and beyond. It is important to keep practicing!

The first few things that you need to remember are the rules for the recall, and these should always be followed. They are:

1. Always call your dog for something good (food, love, a walk on the beach, playtime);

2. Never call your dog for something bad – go and fetch him (trips to the vet, bath time, home time from the dog park); and

3. Never scold your dog when he comes to you (even if you have been standing in the rain calling him for 15 minutes).

The rules make sure that your dog will come to you when called because he knows that something good will happen. It is your responsibility to make sure that something good always does happen when you call him. So, make sure that you call your dog for all the good things, and try to fetch him for the bad things.

And make sure that, even if he takes a long time responding to your call, that you always make a fuss of him (and give him a treat if you have one) when he does come. If you are annoyed with him, you can call him whatever names you would like so long as you do it in a high pitched happy voice.

When your dog is a puppy, he will likely follow you wherever you go, and make sure that he has you in sight. As your puppy grows up, and especially when he starts to test the waters at 6 months, he will become more independent and venture further and further away from you.

The more you can do to train the recall early on, the better.

What happens after the program?

This program has given you the basic tools for training and by the end of it you should be comfortable with the methods of training. You can continue on your own by reinforcing behaviour that you like and teaching your dog other tricks using the methods you have learned.

There is also a wealth of information out there you can use to help you, just make sure you use positive reinforcement! There are even videos on the Internet you can watch on how to teach tricks.

The more time that you spend with your dog the better, and training is an excellent way to build a bond and show off! You can also attend classes if you would like to, or even begin agility or other dog sports. Dog dancing is becoming very popular.

The problems and How to solve them

Everyone worries about what bad dogs do, and here we discuss a few of the typical "bad dog" behaviours that are common problems and how best to deal with them briefly. This section provides help for the following:

Counter surfing;
Digging in the rubbish;
Stealing items (especially socks);
Barking at people/ things/ small children/ bicycles; and
Not coming when called.

Counter surfing

It is important to remember that your dog is a scavenger. If you are lucky enough to have a dog large enough (or clever enough) to get onto the kitchen counter to steal food then there is unfortunately very little that you can do about it. Food stealing is essentially a self-rewarding behaviour.

Which means that your dog gets the reward when completing the behaviour: he gets to eat the food he has stolen. The only way to deal with this behaviour is to eliminate the reward. This can be done in two ways:

Shut the kitchen door; or
Never leave food on the counter

You will find if you never leave food on the counter after a long period of time, your dog will stop expecting it to be there and the behaviour will stop. However, he may relapse so the only certain way of eliminating this behaviour is to make sure that food is not left out unattended.

Digging in the rubbish

This behaviour is almost the same as that of counter-surfing. It is self-rewarding which means that your dog gets a tasty reward (chicken bones, that left-over salad) if he digs in the rubbish. A similar solution is required for this behaviour:

Rubbish should be stored out of reach of the dog

This can be accomplished by storing it above the ground on a platform, or in a closed room. If you find that your dog gets into the rubbish when you leave it out for collection, you can invest in bins with securely fitting lids, or place the bags on an elevated platform.

Stealing items

This is one of the very first things your dog trains you to do! Most dogs learn how to steal things. It begins with items that smell like you being left around (socks are prime examples!).

Your dog will experimentally pick these up, at which point you start yelling at him and chasing after him. Your dog has just invented a game, and it is probably his best game ever!

The way to prevent this from starting in the first place is twofold:

Don't leave items lying around

Try to put your dirty socks in the laundry basket, and the laundry basket out of reach of your dog. If he has no socks to steal, then he wont steal them.

Try to provide him with plenty of other entertainment in the form of toys and chews he is welcome to carry around. Perhaps even have a few that you will play a chasing game with.

Don't chase your dog when he steals something

Even if it is one of your lucky socks. If your dog realizes the fun part of the game (you chasing him) doesn't happen anymore, he will stop. This may not happen right away, but it will happen if you are patient.

So, no matter what he takes, you will have to be sure not to chase him. If he is likely to then sit and chew and swallow your sock, it is posing him a danger, in which case it is best not to leave such items around.

Swap it for a toy

If your dog realizes that the chasing game will no longer happen, but he still steals things, try to swap them for something he is allowed.

Having plenty of toys and chews around should keep him busy and if he brings you a sock, or your slipper (unrequested), then try to give him something else to chew (like a hoof).

Try not to confuse him by having shoes he can chew and having those he can't. Rather stick to dog toys for chewing and all human-related items out of bounds.

Barking at things

Things could include anything here from people in hats to small children. Usually this is down to one thing and that is insufficient socialization. Puppies need to get used to as many things as possible in their first few months to ensure that they are "bulletproof" and not scared by everyday things.

If you ensure that your puppy is exposed to as many new things as possible when he is young, he will be a well-developed and socialized older dog.

You should try to introduce him to at least 100 other dogs by the time he is 1, and make sure that he is used to people of all shapes and sizes (to a dog, children are a different thing altogether) and you should have few problems.

If your dog is aggressive at all, to anyone or anything or to other dogs, consult a professional behaviour specialist immediately.

Not coming when called

This is usually the second thing that your dog trains you to do (after the fun sock stealing chasing game). You are also a bit to blame for this one, and you have probably broken the cardinal rules, which are:

1. Always call your dog for something good (food, love, a walk on the beach, playtime);

2. Never call your dog for something bad – go and fetch him (trips to the vet, bath time, home time from the dog park); and

3. Never scold your dog when he comes to you (even if you have been standing in the rain calling him for 15 minutes).

The recall is easy to train, but you need to do it constantly and make sure that you follow the rules! A few exercises can help with this:

Make your dog come for his dinner

This can be done easily with two people. Divide your dog's dinner between the two of you and stand at opposite ends of the house. Call him between you, giving him a handful of his dinner each time.

Call your dog and then let him go

If you are away on a walk in the park, or along the beach and you call your dog to put on his lead to take him home, he will not want to come.

Continually calling him, putting him on his lead and rewarding him with a treat, and then letting him go again will ensure he doesn't know when it is home time and he knows he will get a treat if he comes to you.

Call your dog for treats

Try to do this regularly, call your dog, give him a treat and then just let him continue what he was doing. This will train your dog (along with the rules above) that coming when called means good things are going to happen.

Conclusion

Through reading this book, and following the four-week course, you should be completely proficient in getting your dog to sit, down and stay. He should also be walking loosely on the lead, properly house trained and happily greeting other dogs and people who you encounter.

You have also learned quite a bit since doing this course, training techniques that you can apply to any trick or behaviour you would like your dog to do. There are a few things that you should remember, no matter if you stop here at this basic level, or go on to become an agility or obedience champion.

1. Rewards should always be used during training. You might start out with one treat every time your dog does what you ask him for a new trick or behaviour, and then move on to a different rewards-based schedule but make sure that you always have treats handy.

2. Remember to build behaviours up slowly. If you would like to train your dog to roll over, you may have to start from the down position. Then roll onto your dogs back, and then try to lure him over. It may take several training sessions over several days. But if you are patient and persevere, you can do it.

3. Remember to always end on a good note. Even if you have just taught your dog to turn the light switch on, you still will want to end in a sit. It is something he can do and get right every time, and you can reward him for that behaviour.

4. Practice! The more you practice the better you will get and the less you practice the more likely your dog will forget the behaviour. So don't forget to keep going and keep practicing.

Be sure to remember that training should be fun for both you and your dog, so take your time and be patient and see what you can accomplish.

Bonus Chapter – Tricks to build that great relationship

This chapter will reiterate much of the exercises that have already been described in this book, but to have an awesome dog, you will need to make sure that you spend time with your dog building up that relationship.

There are quite a lot of things that you can do to ensure this and this chapter will give you some exercises to make sure you keep building that relationship!

Walking

Walking your dog is one of the most important things that you can do with your dog. The time that you spend together is important. Your dog needs the exercise and I am pretty sure that you need it as well. Although some people are extremely busy, you should always make time to walk your dog.

Getting a professional dog walker or your domestic worker to do it will mean that they are building that relationship with your dog, rather than you. If you want the relationship, then you need to do the work.

On-lead walks are great ways to build up your relationship with your dog. He will always need the practice for walking loosely on a lead as each walk will prose new distractions to challenge him to so it properly.

You should make sure that your route is varied; try to avoid going the same way at the same time every day. You may do that every weekday, but see if you can change it on the weekends, for example.

Although dogs love routine, they also need a challenge. You may want to take a new route that goes past a school, or a busy parking lot. But try to challenge your dog to deal with new experiences.

It will also make sure that you build up an understanding of your dog. The more you walk him in this way, the more likely you are to anticipate behaviour. For example, you may learn that when your dog pricks up his ears in a certain way, he will likely have seen something to chase.

Anticipating this can enable you to be able to develop the command and training to stop him. If you would like to do serious heel training, don't do it for the full walk, remember your dog's attention span cannot handle much more than 15 minutes at a time. The walk is also time for him to have a little sniff and get reacquainted with his environment.

Off-lead walks also provide a great opportunity. In the off-lead environment you can play fetch, you can practice the recall and you can provide your dog with the opportunity to play with other dogs.

It also allows for the experience of new situations and it is great if your dog gets to learn not to chase birds and squirrels and that horses and cows should not be barked at. The more you expose your dog to situations like this, the better.

Staying calm

There are some situations in which you will be a little scared. There are times when, on an off-lead walk, you will encounter a very large dog bearing down on your little sausage dog and you will probably panic. The trick is to remain calm.

Your dog will probably greet the new arrival with enthusiasm and start playing. But if you panic, he is likely to pick up on that and also get a little scared and a scarred dog can often respond by being aggressive.

If you are worried that you cannot keep calm, then the best course of action is to ignore your dog. It sounds strange but by ignoring your dog by, for example, engaging the owner of the very large dog in conversation, your dog will probably be fine.

You can apply this is most situations. And you will soon learn the value in staying calm and ignoring your dog. Usually he will be able to then deal with the situation on his own quite effectively provided you have socialized him enough.

There of course are some situations when you may encounter an aggressive dog, in which case you need to try to get your dog out of there (avoid the teeth!). However, you will find that people with aggressive dogs generally keep them on lead or do not walk them at all so the likelihood of this happening is not great.

Ignoring your dog at home can also be good. If your dog falls down the stairs, or becomes scared in a thunderstorm, ignoring him and staying calm is the best you can do. If he is obviously injured after falling down the stairs, then rush him to the vet but if he isn't, pretend nothing has happened.

This makes your dog secure in the knowledge that it wasn't anything to be worried about and will just continue as normal. If you do panic, and run to your dog to check that he is ok, you run the risk of him developing a phobia.

A phobia is difficult to deal with after it has established so try your best to ignore your dog when your instinct is to run to him to see if he is ok.

Training

You may feel, that after you have completed these four weeks, you don't want to continue. That is absolutely fine! Not very many people see the need to train to competition standard; it is just not needed for everyday life. However, training can add value to your relationship with your dog.

Even if you just practice the tasks you have learned in this course for a few minutes every day you are providing that stimulation for your dog and building your relationship.

Play

Playtime also serves to increase the strength of the bond you have with your dog. A game of tug or fetch is a great way to spend time with your dog, as well as making sure he gets rid of some of his energy. A tired dog is a good dog! Rather spend 15 minutes playing tug or swimming I the pool with your dog than he chews up the irrigation system later.

There are also a wealth of different toys and games out there specifically designed for dogs and owners to play together. It is worth having a look at a few of them.

You may even want to keep your dog busy with a treat-dispensing game. These will allow you to get some downtime whilst your dog is busy on his own. Kong toys stuffed with treats are a great way to keep most dogs busy.

A hoof filled with peanut butter (with no added salt or sugar) usually will keep most dogs busy for half an hour or so.

For dogs that don't destroy things, a plastic cool drink bottle makes an excellent toy. All you do is empty it, rinse it with clean water and then let it dry. Cut a few holes in it big enough for treats to fall out of it.

Then fill it with a handful of treats, close the lid and give it to your dog. He will likely spend a great deal of time figuring out how to get the treats out and rolling it around. This is a great way to keep a dog busy and using his brain.

If you found this book helpful, would you be kind enough to leave a review for this book on Amazon?

Thank you and have a nice day!

Sally Kilpatrick

CPSIA information can be obtained
at www.ICGtesting.com
Printed in the USA
BVHW032317141122
651902BV00007B/962